TABLES

Tables

Poems by
DABNEY STUART

PINYON PUBLISHING

First Edition: 2009

Pinyon Publishing
23847 V66 Trail, Montrose, CO 81403
www.pinyon-publishing.com

ISBN 978-0-9821561-1-7

11/
/2011

Some of the poems in this book have previously appeared in:

The Gettysburg Review – "Kungälv, Sweden: Christmas, 1938" (Vol. 16 #4, Winter, 2003).

Hampden-Sydney Poetry Review – "Cobblers," "Survivors" (Winter, 2006); "Focus," "Joachimsthal" (Winter, 2007).

The Paris Review – "Gifts" (#172, Winter, 2004)

Poetry – "Fine Time" (as "Finding Time") (Vol. CLXXXIII, #1, October, 2003); "Talon" (Vol. CLXXXIII, #5, February 2004); "Traveling Light" (Vol. CLXXXVII, #2, November 2005).

The Roanoke Review – "Joints," "Monks 3" (as "Monks") Vol. XXX, Spring, 2005).

Southwest Review – "Primitive Weaponry" (Vol. 92, #3, 2007).

TriQuarterly – "Yucca Mountain," "Monk" (first poem in the "Monks" sequence) (#129, 2007).

The Virginia Quarterly Review – "The Light the Magician" (Vol. 83, #2, Spring, 2007).

The Alhambra Poetry Calendar: "Dreamcatcher" (Alhambra Publishing, Bertem, Belgium, 2009).

for Sandra

Contents

The Word withdraws from the first will to recognize it as transformed Nothing.

– Northrop Frye

...let those fires,
Which shall consume the world, first make it tame.

– George Herbert

GIFTS

Nothing alive can keep us as we go.
The end loves all the doors that close away.
We may embody what we never know.

I hear a song, my ear is tuned its way;
I doubt another soul is listening so.
How much of this is here I cannot say.

Today is no more *now* than what we flow
around and out from, the tender play
and nuance fading above the lines. So

Yeats began his last drama in a graze
and stupor, longing inverted, the show
staged on the pallid air without a trace

of author or audience. A shadow
has more concoction. Implicit Mallarmé
felt syllables in a senseless undertow

pulling him toward a music time's gray
undoings leave no markings for. Low-
ing of cattle, bellwethers. Paul Klee,

his hand brushing his son's shoulder as though
to draw thence his dancings, tried to allay
the long wait in a box, virtuoso

toying with angles. Pudgy Joan Miró
made floral epididymides sway
and swim in a gathering overflow

of plasma and grist. No one can betray
gifts so immanent, so trimmed, their piano
forté thinning even as a rainbow

imagines itself without mist. Unsay
what you can. Out in the desert Rimbaud,
king of kings, hawks baubles, and the echo

rises against the sun's hammered tray.
He doesn't distinguish, nor does yesterday.
The end loves all the doors that close away.

AIR TIME

Music, which is ethereal in its being,
and...terminates in pure essence,
nevertheless in its play...is full of
trepidation, terror, potentiality,
and sweetness.
                    – George Santayana

Relentlessly suppliant,
monks sing to a high choir,
their echoes fading in the cloister
for days, counterpoints to the next chant,

lingering modulations of lives
pressed into the fine grain of voices
raised to the blankest of blank places.
Regardless of what one believes

the spirit enhances silence,
giving it play within its tendencies
as if its innate fading conveys
a listening, a resilience,

a lifting in the stark drift to space.
Out there bodies also conduct
long disciplines, gas and ice and rock
cavorting in the singular stress

of unnumbered galaxies, quantum
choirs enacting measureless music,
susurrae working a soft magic
across the imponderable systems.

This isn't a Ptolemaic tune
or tuning – more like the sound of light
in friction with itself, resonate,
as a being can carry within

many strains to one integrity.
So the monks, inconstant but faithful,
release their chanting to the faithful
place of blank voices, the big empty

drifting apart, belying the force
that holds them to their knee-breaking stone.
Their song defies it, too, a motion
of emptying, gone without recourse,

animation and paean that flies
for the sake of its own lost rising,
sung to vanish like an open string's
sound vibrating to the touch air plays,

an afterthought, a casual drift.
It hovers briefly in the niches
of the cloister's walks, hardly touches
the prismed light spun in the choir loft,

leaves as a farewell leaves its speaking
in its own name. The remaining breath
the monks sustain is an aftermath
of their mown longing, the song's breaking

out and away. They are always left
with it, this respiration. It haunts
the hours they do not sing, discontents
they whisper to themselves, a fine thrift

rehearsed in the temper of their cells
until, in the pre-dawn bells, they rise,
matins stirring in their lungs, a mist
forming, habit that calls and impels

at once. Their voices will clarify
this strain in the invariable dream
that hardly takes a shape, an anthem
opening, blooms on the airy tree.

TRAVELING LIGHT

Moving through still time, its opposite,
it creates no friction. They are both gifts,
one the infinite eye of the needle
the other threads. Occupies.
Emptiness is full of itself,
a neverair, the lens for being.
In the long way of this place,
the afterthought of gasses becomes
what we tune in, its tickless
preoccupation and amaze our present.
If such light made a sound
it would be as if the wide spacewind
formed a bell of itself,
and a smaller wind within, and rang.

THREE RINGS

His life fell open so he could see almost everything.
Since no one else was telling his story, he had to continue.

When the last lending drops away, the audience would gasp.
He would hear it from ear to ear. Was it an expression

of surprise or shock or repulsion? Or awe? Or fury?
Standing undone before himself, he didn't ask.

He was developing his sentence, feeling his way
through its density, its easing into itself.

No diligence or foresight, not even an incisive friend,
could have prepared him for the shifts of his life.

Probability was a mask the clown at the circus wore.
The Tomorrow family spun between the trapeze swings,

clock hands gone haywire. I have taken too little care
of this, he thought. But how could I have done otherwise?

Carrying my dead daughter about this desert, listening
to the sand groan and the pitiless birds practicing

for their recital *Who knows? Who knows?* their calls falling
into my ears like rinds into a beggar's bowl.

Was it really a circus? Was the clown in costume?
How could human bodies rotate like airplane props?

What went on in their minds when they slept?
Performers – the end of evolution, fear's face,

quantum jerks of the psyche heated and reheated,
orbits of loss and panic and flight and nothingness

fading imperceptibly into the starlost,
vacuums answering themselves with light.

If the last looped raggedness of my life could fall off
I would reveal everything. I could surrender

my ticket, settle into my seat, look forward
to delight and awe and repulsion and shock and fury.

I could shuffle buttons and redeem my children.
Here's rue. Here's charity. Here's what I came for.

JOINTS

You strum my shoulder, as if to draw music
from the infraspinatus, the bell curve
of heft and bearing. It bows toward your hand

as a cat's back lifts to an incipient caress.
We shoulder our burdens, we put our shoulder
to the wheel, we work shoulder to shoulder;

young Atlas bore the globe on his, with less finesse
and wit than one might wish, yet was able to stand
for his story. It's an odd jointure of sinew and nerve
to run your fingers along so gently, seeking music.

My friend Ezekiel roams the boneyards forever,
singleminded, serving the fundamental gist
of the joint: it not only connects this bone

to that bone both ways, it also enables
the rigid to roll and rotate, Astaire to be loose
as a goose; with Marceau and Hines on the loose

we can bear better the periodic table's
dark, imperious secrets, its ingrown
terror. At Los Alamos the physicists
danced when it seemed their work would last forever.

Some of my other friends are less immune
than Ezekiel to the whims of assembled man.
Miró's incendiary charges delight the young;

they float like particles in the eye of God,
deciduous orbits decaying with a half-life
beyond dimension, affecting if not his life

then perhaps his vision. It is, in fact, near God
Paul Klee sought a place. He would have painted on dung
had it been a more stable medium. Cézanne
painted on water. It proved immune.

Your fingers slip along elbow and wrist and knuckle,
apparently not caring where they hung out. I suspect
they would be happy with any old joint – the back

alleys of the toes, the popliteal's sultry corner,
the sally-forth of the joint that is not
really a joint, pendulous, ready or not

with its chain reactions, Little Jack Horner's
plum charged with the future. Its agaric shape lacks
the comforting, mammary swell of the circumspect
cloud over Trinity. You kiss my wrist and knuckle.

We persist: Zeke and Joan, the two Pauls and you – friends,
the present tense, always, our immersion in
the welter called God, no person, the planet's roll

and rotation, nova, part and parcel, here;
lists without verbs, essence of hope and being;
red burning spits, sapience, coil of being

and essence. Where we hang out, sphere within sphere,
all guesswork, loose in the mind's infinitesimal
pitchblack scurry to counter itself. Connection
among the last extremes you'd think could become friends.

Zeke harps on that, his trials, the liminal expanse
through which he roams, humming, implying a tune
might eventually rise from his composures.

He taps you on the shoulder, smiles, complicit.
Elegant, fine-boned Laura Fermi must have touched
Enrico like that uncountable times, touched

him, too, where he thought about the exquisite
blossoming of the actinides, prolonged exposure
to which mars the fingers. Outside, I hear a loon
cry, while the universe infinitely expands.

This can be played over and over, these same notes,
these procedures, lines under compression,
moving from the mind, touched, to the fingers

which release them into the figures of thought.
It's what fingers do, touch the imagination's music
into the world that it might be heard, music

bereft, nostalgic for the silence it issued from, caught
in its bearing signs. The most poignant singers,
hearing those origins, know life is fission.
They are – Bohr, Miró, Frisch, Joliot, Cézanne – making notes.

MARROW

The refugees murmur
to their inner settling,
their voices gone
almost to bone.

Their murmuring is the rhythm
they walk in, the measure
the dust from their feet
rises by.

It disperses, drifting
over the tracks, through the oaks
and sycamores, toward the river.
It, too, settles.

The hawk that soars
above them, wearing its trail
in air, another distance,
sees what it needs,
dives.

TRIALS

If I weren't someone else, would I talk to myself?
I wish I had Zeke's range, his focus –
a scientist's absorption. But these fences
fence me in; I rehearse the final interview,
or at least *an* interview, incessantly virtual.
Rehearse, a rut. The words change the bubble's
shape they float in, and rearrange. A little trial,
foolish and fond even at its most acerbic.
I'm the prosecutor, always defending myself.

A new character appears, General Funf.
He is a sound, empty as gas.
What is he five of ? Why does he strut?
Bechested with medals, abrupt, presiding.
I couldn't save her I tell him, all of him;
My only daughter, and I rubbed her feet.
He is miles high, off his rocker, a rank goose
holding me by my collar between his thumb and forefinger.
I say *I remember* when he shows me her picture.

These must be the cliffs of fall, these hobbled selves, hung up,
citizens of the mock rejoinder. One of them used to hide
in the rack under an Airstream trailer. What good is he
as an apologist? I call him Sir Philip.
Occasionally he gives me a rhyme, like *tables*
and *enables*, but for all his urbanity
he doesn't consort much with the rabble.
In spite of his theorizing, he could be Roy Rogers
riding the ridge where the west commences.

Today I set up my joint stool in the desert.
Surprise. *Mesa*, a mountain with the top sliced off.
Zeke, Sir Philip and I are the grillees,
General Funf arraigning upon us
from his eminence. Sir Philip shows the best balance
on the joint stool, but his answers, courtly, suave,
float off in the winds as if someone else
were listening. Perhaps my father, freed by the sonnet,
keeps a watch in the high country north of us

where the peaks bloom year round. Someone cracks his cheeks
and lets loose a low, bean-charged rumbler you could
mistake for thunder if you're big enough. King-sized.
A question for the ages. None of us replies, but Sir Philip
whispers something about his girlfriend Blanch barking
at him, and oppressed nature having a hard heart.
General Funf disperses, the nth factor
of himself spread into the sky, a discrepancy
devoutly to be wished. He leaves me the photograph.

I'd have preferred he gouge out my eyeballs
with his free thumb and forefinger and hang them
on a piñon for the buzzards to feast on.
I could accompany Ezekiel as a blind apprentice,
learn to finger bones like Marsha Ogilvie,
tell who'd died of what, who had ridged femurs
so a passing wind could make music on them.
Tibia tunes, too. The notes of life marking time,
a way off, in the distance there, charming:

Neanderthal noodling one can make history of.
I have tried looking in my heart to write this,
according to instructions, but hypertension
and elevated cholesterol have muddied the source.
Logic tells me this is why I talk to myself,
but I distrust logic almost as much as I distrust words,
and I am someone else besides. When the wind blows
through the Sierra Oscura, the court convenes,
or I hear it convene, deliberating, which means

putting their voices in the scales to see
how they weigh out. O self-engendering verdicts,
my company, I cry you mercy. I am surrounded,
the sounds of language knocking on a door,
cells dividing, another world. Is it better
to draw the curtains and be quiet? To whisper
sweeter nothings than these? To love, or learn to love
the murmurings that never form a name,
their contentment with the bufferings of air?

MONKS

He bends to the manuscript blossoming
under his pen, amorphous roseate

haze rising from the gesture his fingers make,
smoke from a magic lamp even older

than the gnosis he is moved by, moves from,
inditing, word by illuminate word,

the truth hidden forever in the letters –
the very ones – he so diligently sets down.

He's not writing history – no one can
do that. He's loosing its air

into the air we breathe, trembling
with the wonder incipient in an eyelid

or the rind of a lime. He feels the fire
and dolor in his golden capitals,

his pen releasing blossoms,
the flameless flowers of Edo –

the darker ages become a bursting ground,
craters of mindfire, the running crowns

of thought, essences rising
above the water where the names burn.

WINTER LIGHT

It evens, noon and twilights
an array of sameness.
To enter it is to conceive
its deepening, to gather its surface
into the body, unbroken.
Even the nearest touch is an offing,
space in the iris –
how far sight can bring inward
the gray spread of the world.
As if the lungs were a honeycomb
where shimmers of air hum to themselves,
breath releases a sweetness
into this doldrum, promising itself.

KUNGÄLV SWEDEN: CHRISTMAS, 1938

1.

Otto Frisch was not thinking of the long-range
firefall, fallout, though for an instant
during his walk in the snow with Lise –
the two of them warmed by intimation,
the seethe of an idea, Bohr's droplet,
a dwarf dumbell dividing – the bright prospect
of such reaction may have stunned him,
turned his mind for a spun millisecond
into its own ground zero: an image,
a shockwave of exuberance, a bane.

2.

They took tea often that week, Lise Meitner
and Otto, in the small inn under the cliff.
She spilled a little sugar on the linen
cloth as she bore it in the miniature spoon
from bowl to cup. His fingers fretted
the woven surface as if they hankered after
the keys he was so expert with. Families
of talent, nurturing, full of humor. Lise
has come here from Stockholm, her exile.
Otto's father will be released from the camp
in the new year. Things fall apart. She walks
in the snow beside him skiing across King's
River. A pad of paper in her purse,
innocent as thought, waits for their drawings,
the rough drafts of the mind's new rendering
of the appalling core of things, of itself.

VOWEL SOUNDS

Names are nothing.
– W. B. Yeats

1.

That's true. They are thinner air
than the air that absorbs them,
so refined that the voice releasing them
almost palpably from the mouth
feels no loss in their going.

It's not a matter of care
for place or person, or even the idea
of presence, for we love those and their idea
in zygote silence, in the pith
of their unspeakable being.

2.

What names did Curie, Meitner, Bohr
murmur in secret, thoughts dark
in their grooves, not even thoughts, inchoate, dark-
er than God's minutest pocket, mute
as an ovum, unsplit?

They are part of our atmosphere,
those broken, decisive thoughts, minds'
smithereens reflecting nature and our minds'
careening, the particles' dispute
with one another as nonchalant

as Fermi's finger probing his ear.
They scattered, incidence
eliciting unpredictable coincidence,
as if a marble, colliding,
could deflect a wrecking ball.

3.

They unveiled the stricken core
of everything, using the echoes
of numbers as a guide to the echoes
of matter. They found it eliding
beyond sense, even the siren call

of imagination. Or desire.
Whatever elemental name
they chose for one mystery derived from a name
for another, ancient,
unplumbed: *uranium,* king

of the mountain, first sire
and son of Chaos; *proton,* simply
first, a hint that the whole neverknow is simply
a progression. Is there no end
to that, or the ghostly spinning

4.

in all nuclei, as pure
and inaccessible as the secret
frictions that make each family a secret,
discrete mob that may fly apart
at the slightest pressure?

We seem to endure
that, too, and the interior
selfscatter that mirrors the exterior
extremes it finds in its heart
and head, and cannot measure.

TALON

From the ledge of my cell window last night
Pero the dreamhawk took two avocados
I had set there for him. It was a bargain,
but it isn't clear what I received in return.

Pero is masterful. It is rumored
he will slash a person's forearm for no reason.
I believe this. I have seen his eye in sunlight.
It is like no other dream in the kingdom –
a talon, an archangel of a lost art.

After he took the avocados, after
they disappeared from the sill, my window
eased open even farther, seemed to drift
away and become air, become a voice
which had not spoken with clarity
for a long time. I imagined it
inherent in the air, but of this other
substance, also transparent, yet chilled,
brittle, intransigent. It would need to be broken
many times before it would be fine enough
to be indistinguishable from the air it sings.

To be faithful in a few things.
To be thankful for small favors.
To be undone by the unlikely, the modest.
To be alien in the garden, to look up.

FOCUS

No matter the acreage of Zeke's bones,
the conclusion here defies even the most devious
augury. There are never hints what his next
assemblage might decide about its future,
                                            but at least
no one who has been through what it takes
to get here will ever be a fanatic again:
do not consider the lilies of the field –
they toil not, neither do they spin,

nor do they seek refuge in the rivers
whose banks are burning. A man from a village
saw a cloud over the distant city.
It was neither red nor yellow, a huge cloud

rising angrily – it defied description.
On both sides of the main cloud smaller clouds
spread out like a golden screen. I have never
seen anything so magnificent in all my life.

So words spread their own screen, and speech
alone doth vanish like a flaming thing,
a thing so fleeting the scars of its burning
are invisible and take no time.

Ezekiel's system isn't closed,
yet the spread goes on; without his attending,
its endless continuum would seem
an entropic scramble, the tip of old Chaos:

the undoing of so many cleanses us
of misgiving, graces our borrowed dust,
releases us to touch, its surety,
                                    its long lost.
In agony, we turn to those we love;
lying alone we spin out the filaments
seeking them – son, wife, daughter, friend, the one
that anchors. But no one's there at the flash

22

of the first certainty. The threads of the web
curl and return, as hair on the forearm
singes at the edge of the range's flame;
they loop it all back – our panic and longing,

our drive into the large body of the world –
into this coalescence of simple light,
this present,
                    nowhere
we could have reached without the going,
another closing away, the body

that never leaves itself drawing the whole
expansion back into its uncanny stillness,
more dense and impervious than any nucleus.

COBBLERS

Patience. Someone is listening
to your needle's hum. But if you weren't lacing
that upper down, perforating the welt, absorbed,

you could undo this button, this little button.
Your thread's coherence has the serenity of old trails
leading somewhere, its coils drawn tightly

into a seamless seam. Isaac Newton at birth
was small enough to fit into a quart pot.
From there to decades spent gazing

into a retort is a short trip. Unpublicized.
Unmentionable, his hunched obsession
with the stone that transmutes, that burns

the imagination's light into matter's
hidden orbits. Mix. Reconfigure. Spin –
the galaxies within earth as forbidden

as the one Copernicus fiddled with.
Time to light the lamp. The fine music
your thread lifts from the leather rises like mist,

a faint version of the wind playing over
a rack of Ezekiel's vertebrae. This feather stirs.
An angel listens. Into deep space the thread loops

its unreasoning intimation. Being a small man
born in a cold place, it's no surprise Sir Isaac
spent his life bent to a furnace, distilling,

imagining a green lion munching the sun.
Causality was a needful proposal
to the world, which it accepted, the disguise

behind which he sniffed and rooted, little dreaming
U238 was dividing itself, nameless, by its own fire:
all the time the lion was chewing,

and pulled out a plum. Granular perception –
stitches in time, in the void, sewing nothing.
So our gentle cobbler – who works from the actual

outline he draws around his clients' feet,
standing on cardboard in 2009 –
puts his newly finished shoes on the sill

and blows out the kerosene lamp.
The nuclear powder is undisturbed.
This body I carry may still be alive;

Zeke can hold his feather
beneath her nostrils again.
I draw a line between this star, and this,

imposing my centaur, my scorpion,
punching holes, entertaining, riddling in the dark.
The other cobblers practice their random sleep.

THE WIND SINGS, THE WIND DIES

Light blades, nothing
to think of, chance
forking its maze –

    e pluribus unum
    and the unworn skins.

I climbed the steps
to the stone niches above Sweetwater
Canyon, sat in one and listened
to the wind sing across its mouth.
I was a still clapper
in a bell cut into a cliff's side,
as close to no one
as the wind's dying.

Across the canyon
hawks shaved the sky
above the stark cottonwoods,
their trails mapped
in an elation of air.

Somewhere a Navajo woman
sits before her loom in the sundust,
making a pattern of all this.
Her shuttle's hush
blends with the fibers.
My absence is a thread in the weave.

MONKS 2

A great seclusion and darkness are
requisite for…organic patterns to
take shape undisturbed.
                    – George Santayana

But what shape? My heart, extracted live,
flopping its last throes on the steel table,
the veins' blind cargo flecking the sheen:
is this Onanistic orgy what it comes to?
The honourable Japanese tradition
of white kimono and ceremonial sash,
of the thousand-year-old dagger
sheathed in the hand-carved duplicate of its handle:
what is its aftermath? No films show that –
only the starched eyes of the suicide,
his honed intention. The camera rises
from the autopsy, too, when the pathologist
incises the chest. We are left
to imagine strata it's not decorous to see.

We're used to saying *He wears his heart on his sleeve*,
and *Her heart is an open book*, keeping the fable
somehow separate from the fact. What *do* we mean
by *a heart of gold*, or *a hearty stew*?
We have heart-to-heart talks, and our passion
cries *With all my heart!* Caught off guard, we blush
still, our hearts on fire. Words are a great wagger
of the dog. Bent to these as to a sun dial,
measuring shadow while the light is out,
I drift off, dazzled. From the manuscript's
underside shapes glow, layered, their disguises
burning away – they become what they are, the gist
of their exposure. I can't imagine
what it isn't possible to see.

In the heart's utter darkness, the dense trove
of its cloister, a little trouble
can hide for decades – a tic in the vein,
an arterial wall you could see light through
if you could detect so small a flaw in the pattern
taking shape in the pitch black – keeping its own wish,
being off true, untiming, a hair trigger
tuned to misfire and make a public shambles
of this most private life, this beat and counter beat.
It isn't difficult to imagine
this, though it is impossible to see
it coming in the welter from the blind side,
the inside, most intimate of traces
biding its moment in the shy palimpsest.

CONVENTIONS

I want to tell Sir Philip
    it's not the heart, at all,
        but even though I'm whispering in his ear
I can't tell if he hears me.

There's a man coming later
    in the century, a bricklayer,
        who will transform your shabby house in the country
into a mansion the mind builds

myths in. You will become
    a legend of bravery,
        courtliness and wit, which I've fallen for
as I fall for any turn of phrase

that illuminates the way
    language can grace itself,
        seem to build a life from the ruinous
tumble of its little pieces.

He must know it's not the heart.
    He's not listening because
        he doesn't need to, knowing convention
rides its own fade into blandness.

Even the Muses were
    conventional, spume flicked off
        when neither side of the bicameral mind
whispered to the other,

turning outward in fear
    and ignorance and habit,
        a sort of radar listening for the blip
of space's presumed voice.

Was Sir Philip one of the first
      to talk to himself, to figure
      his interior mumbling in the old guise
of invocation, and suspect

something? By the time Marvell
      made his Israelites refer to him
      from the deep grasses of Appleton meadows
it was foregone: space *is* a void,

and the corpus callosum
      the membrane shimmering
      with our most precious speech and longing.
I imagine Sir Philip,

hearing no muse, hardly more
      than a child the night before
      his death at Sutphen, lining up his icons
on a rock beside his kip:

an ebony statuette
      of an old man, lean as the desert,
      with his hand plunged into his head, thinking
his fingers; a dreamcatcher,

its malachite center
      dusted with starshine; a shatter
      of glass from Penshurst, the color of blood
thinning into water;

perhaps a phrase burned
      into a scrap of leather,
      too much like jazz to fit into a sonnet,
too opaque for the queen's

syntax, or Sir Philip's
      decorum. These were his
      traveling penates set on a stone
level with his eye

before sleep. They are what
        I love him for, why I call
        his name now and then in this echo book,
cheering myself, why he outlasts

General Funf. He ticks
        into the early crawl of this
        century, new brackets to violate,
edges to spill over, orbits

to leap out of. His take
        on predictability
        is to disappear so far into it
no one notices

when he's gone; I hear him leaving
        all the time, or stealing
        time from one measure and giving it
to another, practicing

a more fluent music
        than he preaches, neverair.
        Together in that. Composed.
The brink of listening.

SURVIVORS

We may trust Nature to guard her secret.
                            – Frederick Soddy (1904)

What does it mean that a man or a woman continues?
Persists.
One day Madame Curie digs pitchblende, her fingers marbled,

and years later sets before guests a centerpiece,
a tube of light
glowing with its own decay, lighting her hands,

their advanced degree, *inflamed* Rutherford said,
a celebration
of luminosity and time's inertia.

Is time the only inorganic light?
The only medium not a medium?
An allowance? A facilitation?

Doctor Hachiya remarks one morning shimmering leaves
reflecting
sunlight against the shadows in his garden;

fifty years later he dreams of an eyeball, naked,
hopping
from a girl's hand into the sky where it hovers

above his head, a meditation, searing,
the way light
veins him, a paralysis, yet here

he is, writing in his diary, burned skin hanging from
his memory
like a kimono, like potato peels, his pen moving.

Movement without progress, a writing into –
scoring of the rock, a holding
between, likening, sustaining pitch.

A poet lists toward a spill of light beside him –
stoneflare,
a second sun – stark

diamond stun on floor and wall and cornice, an accident
he survives
by deflection, by sitting there. What else has he done

besides being adjacent, feeling the veer toward light
no one enters,
a dark sheer of absorbing matter

becoming visible only as it cools, milliseconds,
blinding,
without precedent. What *is* this being?

It can sit still, yet continue.
Amid the world's reshaping, it persists.
It is there when we say tomorrow, and when we don't.

WHAT DR. HACHIYA COULD HAVE DONE

I became a pitiless person
– Hiroshima survivor

One hard morning he heard
voices fall, a choral shattering
like stained-glass blown, splintering,
into the wind. His heart murmured,
Something something. A response.
He spoke, and it was the same sound
diminished until it became
the other side of sound.
The world, it was not the same
world; he carried two extremes
of fallen voices through it.
He could put each one into a burlap sack
and tie a sack to each end of a pole;
he could put the pole across his shoulders
and balance the sacks as he walked.
He could walk up the levelled road
to the top of the hill, balancing
the voices in their sacks, and stand there.

WHAT HE DID

He stood there,
the voices fallen into their two nothings.

He was unfit even to look for sacks
or the material to make them.

He imagined himself walking the road,
the weight of the pole across his shoulders.

VOCATION

...whether they listen or not...
− condition repeated in *Ezekiel*

Do you ever want to just throw it up?
I ask Ezekiel. Doesn't work for its own sake
wear you down after a while? Don't you stop
sometimes and look up at the boneless waste
and wish you could disperse into its gasses?
I'm your only audience and as much
as I depend on you even I'm not here
all the time. He answers *Yes*. And *No*.
Depends he says. *And cancel these italics.*
They make my voice look like an excrescence.
The other parts of your counterpoint
don't seem to mind, and it's especially fitting
for Sir Philip and his la de da, but I'm...
well, unsuited for such singling out.
Anonymity isn't an italicized condition;
I'm trying to blend in, not to be called on again.
I never think of throwing it up, but I like
your image: all those bones, haphazard, rising.
Think of the *whoosh* and *whirr*; talk about counterpoint!
It would outBach the whole Bach family.
And how stunning it would be for my backlog
to unearth its clandestine discipline.
A spray it is to delight the mind's eye.
It sure beats space trash, or an explosion −
Old Plum with its eye of fire −
bones in orbit, bonestars, people imagining
again, connecting, making up constellations.
The resurrection of the body! Beats
the Chebar Canal, that huge cloud of flashing fire,
globed in a radiance, and in the center of it −
in the center of the fire − a gleam
as of amber, and figures coals burned around,
torches moving as the figures moved,
the figures themselves torches, solar, flaring.
I won't describe the figures, but they thrived
as if fire were their element, their cheer and relish,
the wine and vermicelli of their souls.

My summons one time when I did look up.

A version of Dr. Hachiya's dream.

One of God's eyes.
                          Here (oops) he says, pushing
a metatarsal at me. Hold this. Think of it
as a lightening rod, a ground for forces
gathering, the most farfetched congregation
of what some other poor cobblers
dug up over time and strung together
as the periodic table. What we're made of.

SEAR

It's tempting to say he doesn't need me,
but Pero and I are as mutual
a drift as the tectonic plates.
Without me his far cry and the kingdom
his talons mark on the sill
are hardly footnotes to the stories
of drastic awe told in the caves cut
into cliffs above the sweetwater dark.
He doesn't tell me I must change
my life, only live it, and even that
is a prehensile draw in my gut.
Speech is the shadow of a dream
between us, a dewclaw, nothing
more than the scant word I leave
for him now and then to commemorate
the bitter hour, its sear on my tongue.
He carries me into my anger
so far all of my pieces fuse
into the fierce eye of his profile,
a sealing.

STRONG FORCES

According to legend, the pelican
fed her young with blood they pecked from her breast.

Too many sacrifices? An image
of all nurture? No matter how rapid

any fire is, it is still staccato –
all those insistent beaks piercing the skin.
Human babies devour piecemeal, too – their zest

pre-empting the outer world entirely. *Id*
Freud's translators called it, language

pecking monosyllabically a new
order, stacked, as they all are, on previous

ones – a tower of babble, or Blake's ladder
to the moon. We have no adequate measure

of what has crumbled to make room for this.
Man who let fart in church sit in own pew

Confucius said, his colon and bladder
perforate from too much thought and pressure.

Appetite he went on, muttering. *Consequence.*
Terse, as always – perhaps delighting in it,

remembering his own mouth around the teat,
the good fortune of mammals. Pelicans,

nonetheless, survive, a kind quintessence
suggesting also the rare, indefinite

patience of recovery. Nourish, retreat,
heal – pain an early gift from the young: a dance

whose formality enables both passion
and restraint. Love well what you must leave? –

easy for Will to write, but what we must
let go is everything, including our children
whatever their distance, and he gives no hints

how we might accomplish *that*. The rhyme is *grieve*.
We have no claim on any of our possessions,

Santayana opined, not even our lives. Dust
to dust, another quintessence.

Do all patterns inhere in this grainy chase?
Logic disperses into it, and coherence.

Our finest instruments record the signs
of its energy, the results of prescience,

or superior guesswork. *Without a trace*
we say of what vanishes, an inference

from the air around us, friendly confines
we draw into ourselves, making no more sense

than a flame blown from a candle, but atomic
still. Whole families can disappear

into it, particulate energies
scattered past the most sensitive detectors.

Heat, radiation, vibes register, but whose?
The mind creates the terms of its desire,

yes, and perspective alters motion, magic
(like this) deflecting us from the more direct force
of loss, the pitch and fell of dark, its promise.

MONKS 3

It's a maddening habit they have,
illuminating manuscripts. I don't mean
the golden tropes that blossom at capitals

as if the words couldn't lead somewhere
by their own light, but the commentary
that runs in their minds, overtoning the text.

They would above all be clear, coax
the text clear, gentle the wispiest hint
in the quietest, most remote niche

into the open web where the mind's breeze
might ruffle it as one. Their calligraphy
in the guttering dark spins toward this,

each word wanting to join the next,
an unbroken skein for the mind to weave with,
reweave with. Troubling. A farthing dropped

in the mud. A year's drag of sciatica,
an offering. Drought in the refectory
garden felt as light. A discipline

inclining. Refrain. The soul designing
its shadow music, blooming through the nib.

THE WHOLE SHOW

The magician whips the bright cloth
away, showing his empty fingers
tuning themselves; on the little
table before him stands a mirror,
a bird gone from it.
In the midst of polite applause
a sound scratches from the dark
gathered in the balconies *Here*
and a flutter ensues, the theater
riddled with it. The magician,
his face pale as a dune,
vanishes under his cape,
a dry puddle on stage. Disconcerted,
the audience straggles out.
In the empty residue, space,
a black birdlike creature
lands on the abandoned cape,
kneads it, settles. There's nothing
remarkable about the eyes
it aims toward the deserted seats,
the ceiling, nowhere,
except the absence of memory.

AIR

The voice carrying on
has nowhere but here to go;
this air it disperses into
weaves with it, grows richer
for its absorption. And the sound,
lingering, gives its new echo
a teasing overtone,
tempting the strain of desire
to vanish altogether.

It's been a time of splitting.
What time hasn't? – the same old song,
the weave I overhear
as I shuttle its counterpoint.
Am *I* richer for that? Compare
balancing on a high wire
with the first kiss of the netting
after the fall that seems so far, so long,
yet is no more than a breath, a faint-

ness opening away. The sky's
the limit, but a feather
won't stir without atmosphere,
our word for only one band
of those quick gasses. If our breath
could dissipate as far as that other
shuttle orbits, what a breadth
of inaudible music, what reprises
flaring beyond their kind!

On a mesa an infant sits,
hardly there, almost transparent,
an inkling of himself becoming
able, a poise, imminent.
As I write him my pen shrinks,
these letters shy of their aiming.
He is no word. He is a thanks-
giving of earth and air knit
of his waiting and my intent.

Made of the same awe and hope,
incredulous at this prospect,
I lift him and gaze up.
I kiss his forehead, his eyes,
cheeks, chest, belly button, the tip
of his penis, his thighs, knees, toes –
all the air his shape gives
me the honor of, the whole aspect
of this body we may live.

We float above the mesa, our
shuttle launched for its own sake
finally, adrift in a lyric
mending. Who absorbs who
in this dance, who's father
who's son, who's bearer, who's born
becomes the name our being whispers
to itself, our return,
the silence we gather into.

FIRES

A little flame in a wild field.
The assumption is it is contained, self-limiting.
It will burn itself out.
But suppose it spreads, turning the field into a wild fire.
The crowns of Yellowstone and Europe topple,
General Funf strides to the pre-eminence of factions.
He commands. He overrides. He is
the essential default − a fist, a handful.
He overtakes the momentum of all voices.
They come out of hiding and ignite his tongue.
Not once does he consider resignation.
His discipline is the discipline of the maw.
A violinist plays on the other side of the globe
but Field General Funf fulfils his destiny.
Silence waits. The future peels away
like sea water from the prow of a destroyer,
yet he doesn't move.
He appears. He speaks. He's gone.
Sunlight exists only as the flash of his medals.

When Funf presides, I curl around my light,
no bigger than a gamete in a field,
a firefly tucked into its fear, part of the dark.
Recession. Nurture. What's left to me.
Old Zeke is far afield, off with the violinist.
Sir Philip vacates, leaving his voice on the piano;
it ticks like a metronome.
My other friends take jobs designing sinkers for Daiwa,
bent to their drawing boards, the lightness of being
flown off with the setae of their dry brushes −
flecks across the moon, starlost.

We imagine the seeds of the ceanothus
that sometimes wait centuries for scarification by fire,
or the Jack pine whose cones must be opened
by fire for the next generation of warblers to nest in.

I am nearly motionless.
The moving fingers move, yes, but having writ
they do not move on. They settle against the pad.
I breathe. My buddy Paul (Klee) said that waiting
is the hardest part. We are ingrained,
Paul and Niels and I, in language;
Niels said *Speech is a clumsiness*
and writing an impoverishment.
I write *move* and *wait*, a pair of blinders
on a mule. What fire scarifies
the pods on imagination's seeds?

Words gather in their seething place,
settle, bide their time,
here and now simultaneous,
an inherent flame.

KEEPING

The figure behind the railing
above me turns to my voice.
I wouldn't call to him
if it weren't time.
His sienna robe settles about him.
Though he is old enough to be my grandfather
I know my face nests in the bowed cowl.
When he straightens, my exact
expression plays like a harmony
in the distance between us.
This is neither mirror nor hologram
but a keeping of each other's promise.
The flesh's absence will be no less
a fine tuning, nothing we haven't heard
before ring in the bell of emptiness.

JOACHIMSTHAL

A German apothecary succeeded in 1789
in extracting a grayish metallic material
from Joachimsthal pitchblende....
He named it uranium.
   – Richard Rhodes, *The Making of the Atomic Bomb*

I know when one's alive and when one's dead.
The fall of a sparrow, the squashed toad, the feather
in the trap, the doe strapped to the car's hood,
all the pretty ones, and the ugly ones

who abound despite the restrictions
on us not to say so: remove a sound
from a language and the fact remains.
Proscribe *weather* and we'd still have weather,

or another fabulation just as good
to cause hurricanoes and like pother
to pour down on our inseminate heads.
Madame Curie appears in a pale gown

as diaphanous as she is, pitchblende
staining the fingerprint she releases, airborne,
blooming luminously. If we could bind
ourselves to our best promise, the bright bouquet

of our curiosity would still ignite
what it kindles, rage through the conifers
and elk-graze above Bandelier,
the gentle and shy and reserved bearing away

the kingdom as randomly as the violent.
This is our planet and the kingdom doesn't belong here.
If earth's the right place for love, it's also right
for everything else mortal and transient...

like the misguided gift refused, leading to madness,
or the skew of a voice – once familiar, nurturing –
toward an uneasy edge, a thinness, becoming tight
as a wire, shimmering with the desire to bless

but instead spilling into disarray
like a cascade done with falling and gone to spray –
all that contradictory murmuring
and splash scattered into pendulous air,

or the almost nothing it originally was
before the unwitting tongue offered it up.
One of its other words was *transform*, which it tried out
for a few nettlesome centuries and then let drop,

a stone into sinking water whose ripples faded
to the edge of grief. The stone itself nudged into the muck
until some shape mistook it for food, a lost crop
of time, and devoured it. New enzymes were needed.

The creature finally spewed it into a net,
sparkling, and the whole trawler fleet could retire
and take cruises to the Caribbean. *What luck*
someone said, and the new word drew explorers

to game shows and the internet. The pastoral
origins of *dollar* participate happily
in this pattern of mute, quantum miracle
that makes it almost impossible to tell

the living from the dead. My wit begins
to turn. Her fingerprint brightens. I'm cold. I'll wrap
this wayward heigh-ho around my shins
and shoulders for old flesh's sake, its little sleep.

YUCCA MOUNTAIN

Give the plant itself a roothold
and it will *undo* a mountain.
Grows down, grows down.
Spreads out its excursions everywhere
like thousand-thumbed chains.
Is no respecter of stone. Shuns picks,
deflects shovels, is immune to moles.
Leaves no surface sign of its campaigns.
A self-rhymed rummaging in the earth,
a fastening, a deliberation.
You'd never guess, in summer
when its white bells cluster on roadside cuts,
rendering the air delicate above
the spearedged spines of its leaves,
how subversive, how replete its boring,
how little water it needs to thrive,
how immune it is.
                    Over the Ghost Dance Fault
the mountain rises, a puny black spine
hardly more than a dune among the ridges
time has rifted up in the desert around it.
The borer – another of Adam's needles –
took only two years to tunnel through it,
an old mole working in th'earth so fast…
and then the vertical shafts to the vaults
for the spent stuff, giving *go down*
a new meaning – yea, verily, giving
deep meaning a new meaning, making
the yucca's tubers seem mere whims in the sand.

Lovers of the wind dancing above,
keeping the planet's time – a slipping of stone
slow as a star's fade – carried all these years
the image of one fault, their ceremonies
tracing it into the air, releasing its crooked
intuition into their own rhythmic webs,
movement that lasted briefly, and is gone,
ghost of itself now, blameless as raw light.
How can they dance again their spidery weaves
when, without the slightest shifting of plates,
new plummets sprout in the wake of the great engines?
Cliffs of fall undreamed. Vibrations crazing
the music to which their bodies ribboned.

It was northeast of here a good distance
I raised my father, gave him away
into the opening mesas and kissed my self
welcome into the airs I have been making
us of, all these decades.
We left our echoes. If you go there
you can breathe them. Our heels click a joy
together. Our motions give a pattern
to their air anyone can join,
invisible leaves from a notebook flying,
ghosting our dance, feathering its voices.

TRANSITION

The old man's head's bowed.
He is in a place strange to him, high desert,
yet he feels he could have been born here.
His forearms drop loosely between his thighs,
his knees spread slightly.
He could be a man waiting
for a prayer to come to him,
or for the number of the year in his head
to turn into a hawk and fly off.
He would make no distinction.
His eyes are partly closed,
the lids hovering toward a clarity.
Or shade. He is the son
of nothing, and its father,
a passage for air and light, a transition.
Words have filtered to the bottom
of a pool whose surface is expressionless
as coal – his mind, perhaps,
if we could know his mind.
He sits on stone under a pleached roof,
head bowed, empty, being born.
If, in the long measure
that has brought him voices, his life,
he hears yet another he will cry *Mercy*
and try to draw them together, more tuning.
But if the hawk has flown,
the prayer gathered into his waiting,
he will hear not even the nothing
he has imagined, or its call.

STARE

Pero has no expectations.
The world is concentric around him.
He includes nothing.

It takes the rare instant
of light angling against the grain
for his eye to sharpen
its dark, singular stun.
It has the relish of a mind
bent on one thing, inward –
bare, unimpressed, a pit.

Yesterday he stared
through the dried light,
the way he flies.

He has gone hungry before.

This morning his appetite
was a scrap left on the sill.

Tonight I give him back
the same blessing, a clarity
for his throat, his calling.

MOTE

I took all my words in the wheelbarrow
and pushed it to the place of ash,
as wide as the Sahara, or a planet
of Sahara. There must have been
fields of life beyond the edges
of that ashwither, but I couldn't see them.
This place I knew was called *Mother*.
Is there nothing but ash and sorrow
in that name? the will that consumes itself
in bitterness and arrest.

None of us is here, not Zeke, not Sir Philip,
not even General Funf, who can be undermined.
What do I call the part of me
who cannot walk out of the Mother?

To be orphaned,
to be left in a basket in the reeds,
to be abandoned on the mountainside
with thongs tied through the Achilles tendons,
to be laid on any doorstep, are all
preferable to the Sahara Mother of Ash.

What is curious is the lure of the place.
Is it still true that of the few citizens
who read Dante most of them settle
in the *Inferno* – preferring its familiarity
and ease to the sacrifice and promise,
the ardor and light, of the other two books?
So I push my barrow here by habit
followed so long it seems like design?
Can I imagine this continuing return
as a scab I pick to open a wound to air?
or as a pelican pecking its breast
to nourish its young? What young?
Dante had St. John in Paradise say
to him *Let me hear how many teeth
Love has to bite you with.*
Is the planet of ash one of those teeth?

With my wheelbarrow, lightest of burdens,
I rise above the desert. I draw its gray borders
in, the slow closing of a lens; the power
of sight runs through all my membranes.
Green fields and copses do indeed appear
at the edges, closing the ashen waste
to the tiniest of shoots, a minuscule
figure hugging itself, a nurture,
the faintest inkling of its own green,
a wrapping of early crowns, layered,
barely discernible now
on the planet of photosynthesis.

Or if the planet of ash remains implacably itself –
not, like pitchblende, both death and transformation –
I take my wheelbarrow, space shuttle,
voice, and launch into the farthest reaches.
The planet of ash diminishes to a speck,
galactic detritus, a smidge of grit in the eye
so small I don't even have to pluck it out.

CONSERVATION

Field General Funf cries *feuer*, pointing
at the peach banana strawberry billowing
of a vast acreage of Yellowstone timber.
We all say *Yes, General* marvelling
at his insight, but the artillery
batteries misunderstand. While
they are recalibrating elevation
and distance, their guns hardly beginning
to rotate ponderously targetward,
Herr Five of Everything calls out *Time*.
We think *What definition!* rehearsing
how we will design his new medal.
The batteries, however, suspend their motion,
random pointers against the flame-pothered sky.
Briefly warmed, Zeke looks up from his work,
noting the flare of complementary responses
to the same terms. Sir Philip, dishevelled,
remembering Sutphen, tries out phrases
on his soundboard: *the motionless barrels*
bind energy, my heart burns, the sky glows
with the guns' yearning. He is positively
clairvoyant, but fails to diagnose
General Funf's condition, his smudge of words.
Layer upon layer, nature's secrets
spewed shamelessly into the forms of language
no two alike can puzzle out.
Does *layer upon layer*, for example,
refer to the sexual exploits of two hens?
Is *spewed* a volcanic metaphor?
(Are all metaphors volcanic?)
Do the delicious adjectives for the fire
in line two suggest a forest of popsicles?
Does *fire in the hole* also mean the outhouse
has finally burst into flames, or is it a way
to fathom the core of fusion? Deeper
plummets have not sounded. The strata
orbiting the center of the earth remain mute.
General Funf fires
and orders an immediate overhaul

of all synaptic ignitions in the corps.
The chain reaction
of his ten-speed baffles him, his day off
passes unnoticed, his lethargy smoulders.
Cooled magma on the big island of Hawaii
is the same color as pitchblende,
as Max Planck's black body.
Love cools, too, and yet in all this wending
no energy is lost, not even in the flare
and fade of phosphorus in the tip of a struck match.

INCLINATIONS

It was all talk.
I see him step to the street
anonymous in the planed light,
turn off, go his own way.
Once we were the same phantom,
teased by each other's voice
toward an overtone of being – his knack,
my need. We have passed the woman
in the slate caftan, her window seat,
leaning slightly, and the sunken man
on the corner, his sheet strewn with petals,
eyes cast away. We have hunkered on
and been rapt by the edges
of sound, stressed, blending – heard
by one of us, glossed by the other.
Each other's margins, we have folded
the corner of a blank page down once
too often, and he walks with no music,
not even the soft scrape of his sole
down the last step, and off. I am
taken by him, as I am always taken.
How I follow is a matter of time,
if I follow, his footfalls gone,
our voices absorbed by themselves
toward a silence we could be blessed by.
It was a calling.

FINE TIME

If I could forget – not the dark backward
and abysm where the shatters of my forming
glint piecemeal, unnameable;
not the eyes of the lost ones, my refugees
turning away into their wandering,
their own selves at last in no time; not even
the knots of betrayal and deceit
I have brought into the world, my missgeburts,
my eels; no, not these but – this present
instant that I stay in yet never am,
no place in time I bide always, pilot of
ambivalence fear laughter vanity igniting
the mind's flare. Words thrive in its mere nothing.
For many miles about there's scarce a bush,
yet the voices of plaint and jubilee
and the mundane eke commend themselves
to vocabulary, rise up and bloom
from the indifferent welter, no matter
who's listening.
What is to me this quintessence of dust
that swirls and forms sounds and contends
with itself in this incessant nowhere?
No one can sort this whirlwind, figure it
with a skill like Ezekiel's, who hearkens
to the air moving over bare joints, hears even
absent cartilage and tendon, and knows.
Puns die because the sense of the self's
palimpsest dies; the wake of waking
throws up too much pain. Ten centuries
of growing consciousness yield nothing, if not
buffers against the strain of that very labor.
So, in a dark like the miner's, and the mole's,
but of no similar purpose, the mind expands,
a camera lens with no shutter and no film
opening to find time in its pure stasis,
the one place we are without being there,
our incoherent gift.

FALLS TRAIL

Bandelier, NM

1.

Names here are dust riven,
thinned in the throat –

firewheel, gilia, greenthread,
ponderosa, cheatgrass,
piñon, ephedra, sage –

breath tremors manyaired,
an otherwise mist dried into light
as suddenly as a thought
spins into another thought.

2.

Dew glints on a piñon needle,
almost low enough to fall
of its own weight before the heat
draws it back.
        Earlier
I stood on the talus slopes,
breathing above the ruins of Tynonyi –
circles within the ring of cubicles
the ancestors hunkered in,
the lost sleeping, a few stones:

we pass through a place always,
no matter how still we are in it,
how long we give ourselves to it.

A hummingbird lights on a twig –
surveys, strikes, returns.

3.

Air opens to less air, outward
to no turning, Frijoles Creek spilling
200 feet below me, a small tracing
mesa-lost, little songs in the rift.

A hawk wheeling sees
a green spine through the strew of dust,

but not the blue-tailed anole
marking a trail on it.

4.

If I were to disperse
into this air, too, whose breath
would we become, whose surrounding?

The hawk's shadow
veers, high up an echo crosses
my mind, its dust stirred.

At this altitude I am
mostly a shallow-lunged old man keeping
somehow a settled pace in the dust
among these presences, their
spare plenitude.

Millennia are no more
than a breeze over this sweetness,
hardly a thin waft in the ghosting.
I could step over
the cane cholla, past
the tuff cones, riddled,
and lean into its edge,
give myself – buoyant
in this late phase of my passing –

to the way of stone cut
by water, down and up
a great emptiness, an embrace.

5.

In the falling air, breath
altogether leaving, I would be
less bodied than a thought.

If the soul's dream is a touch,
then I'm its waking.

The instant I conclude
at the bottom of this, I would
be grateful for everything
that's come here with me,
my plummet's drawn life,

and for the instant, too,

and this place which thins
beyond any expectation
it could survive itself.

He would forget to breathe.
Times he could no longer deflect.
The raw plank door whose edges he feels

in the dark and can't get his fingers
into. On the other side
more edges. Interlocked colonies

of muskrats along the river. Rube Goldberg
plumbing. The shallowest inspiration,
his exhale hardly an echo.

He withdraws even from his icons,
his daily thrive: Mudhead stares
into his pinpoint fear, a clutch

of zeros protruding on its face;
his striated bear, a forest of flaws
pressed into the small stone

he once warmed in his hand,
looks away, eyeless; Old Mosquito
becomes Old Nevermind.

His life, his habit, his compliance,
have chewed him up and spit him
out, a pit of his former self

on the damp cell stone. Cornered.
He's left a trail across the moist surface
of the floor, a series of quirks,

a Rosetta stone. It's a mild loss,
through the only one granted him.
Did I choose? Did I choose? the squiggles

might translate. *Good news. Good news* –
his last traces a matter of accent,
rhetoric. The slick patina

they mar fades in the afternoon sun,
twilight of the odds, no layers
underneath this manuscript.

PRIMITIVE WEAPONRY

The imagination will find the appropriate petard
to hoist itself by. You don't have to kill a king
(any king) or marry with his brother, or starve
millions of serfs through centralized agriculture,
or abandon your baby on a mountainside
with a thong tied through his Achilles tendons,

to put yourself in a position to starve
because you didn't plant a garden. Agriculture
is always local. So is nourishment. Your tendons,
muscles and myofascial sheathes are the petards
that can toss you, unsuspecting, from the mountainside
you didn't train to climb. The mythical king-

dom the man with pierced Achilles tendons
ruled shriveled while he watched. He was his own petard.
His unruly eye-sockets proclaimed him king
of beggars, and the mind that for years had starved
for truth grew lean with wisdom. One mountainside
echoed another. Such trials become an agriculture

of stunted trees and stone. Memories of king-
ship whip them like winds with no direction, starved
for fire. Conflagrations are an agriculture
in healthy forests, thinning, restoring; tendons
of deer and elk grow resilient in their mountainside
survival. The etymology of *petard*

suggests another wind, not agricultural
but just as basic – the kind we break, tendons
and ligaments and bones protecting this petard
that coils through the guts alike of beggar and king.
If released from a strategic mountainside
it can repulse whole armies of believers, and starve

nature of all appetite. Another petard –
used by a nation which still maintains a king –
was called a Flying Dustbin; it bypassed star-
vation by firing spigot bombs, an agricultural
inversion, so to speak, exploding inside
pillboxes, treating unkindly guts and tendons.

When you starve the imagination, its tendons
wizen, and what was king of the mountainside once
compresses into a cultural petard.

But suppose you turn it loose, defy the forms
we try to nettle it with, let it unwind
through the bowels of the earth and the wiles of air,
the infinitesimal galaxies of fission
and guilt, the alphabet of reaction
it makes words of, the granular fracas
we call perception, science in the old sense –
suppose, in fact, what's happened,
and imagination becomes nature's Achilles
heel, or the petard we can hoist it with.

VANTAGE

The other morning,
instead of food
I set my kachina doll, Mudhead,
on the sill.

Pero kept a distance,
watched the sun move shadows
in the vacant eyeholes.

He caught on:
there was nothing
for him to pluck out,
so he balanced on the sill
beside the little statue he loomed over.

He cocked his neck.

Together they look at the world.

SUMMARY

General Funf stirs. Is he man enough
for the job? Even though he can make
the mountain rumble, its crest smoke,
nothing prevents me from replacing
his peaked cap with a slab of butter,
or rubbing my sore butt to call him up
like a genie I sit on when I don't need it.
He is no name for my eels, their traducing
evasions, the coring shapes of their sleep.
They slip in and out of the murk they live in,
compose − sludgelayers, embodiers.
When they relax into their crankcase state
they could irrigate the Sahara mother.
The shadow Jung called them, but The Shadow
just knows, a fit adjutant for General Funf.
Knowledge rides in its nodule atop the spine,
rotating, setting its sights, firing.

                              One of the Pauls
sails in, a genius serving a small breakfast
(an angel bringing what is most desired).
It's not clear if the figure moves through doors
from vacancy into the play of color,
or inscribes itself lightly on a headstone.
It's about to come apart, all its lines
itching to scatter, an air of being
on the verge of giving up, ecstatic...
or an assemblage at the precise moment
all its particles greet each other,
their approximation of form so perfect
another millisecond of gathering
would make a mess of angles, a dissonance:
and this breathing ambivalence is not
an imprecision, but the ease of space,
as if an angel took the shape of a bell
and rang itself into the soul of the world.
I bow to them − Klee, genius, angel −
gifts to themselves, coincidental.

            My brother Joan performs
another rescue into the visceral lurches
General Funf is no match for.
He brings me the true head of a man:
a few edges in the pitch, urgent contours,
an organ with a rudimentary blue
error trying to be an eye, black pupil
smudged – the darkness seeing – and two horizontal
embers full of fire, the space between
them straining to emit words, or their like,
containing more of the black surround
that grounds everything, as if it imagines
a way, different from thought, into its body
of longing, incarnate the inward air.

There you have it, General,
my send-off to your veneer.
Nothing could please me more.
And does – its intimate infancy,
its centering of the low ground, its keeping.

DREAMCATCHER

Only God's most unholy nightmare
could split this — a vision, say,
of the brightest angel at the instant
of his fall, his dark germ breaking,
a mushroom parachute he folds into himself
when he lands, his putrid fire
burning only the eternal cold shoulder
he shrugs at life. A nightmare like that
might clog this fine mesh, shatter its rim,
consume the house and the air of the house,
and the people therein, leaving Ezekiel
more charred emblems for his trove, his tending.

Turned sidelong to words, he considers.
Does he mend, or just assemble,
or contemplate that, a former collocation?
It's all oblique he thinks *the way it comes
at me*, the way the dreamcatcher angles
itself toward the dream's drift that would evade it.

This one, matchless, hangs in the north bay
of the sleeper's bedroom. Its chamois-wound
rim encloses a mesh of arcs, intricately
interlocked, like the wings of a band of angels
seen from above, à la Busby Berkeley;
their tensions and resilience resemble
those of a well-strung tennis racket.
It's four inches across. Three tiny drops
keep their suspended orbits in the net:
one turquoise, one quartz, one silver, all
dancing round the little wedge of malachite
at the center of everything, marking the point
where the best dreams gather, to be dreamt again.
Small beads and feathers dot three rawhide stems
spilling like a beard from the lower edge.

Were this inestimable sifter hung in the long wind
of space, it could tilt and waver for centuries
and pick up nothing of measure. Here its life
riffles with the sleeper's breath, his dredging,
his endless turning among the sortless dreck
that keeps in his mind a fission echoing
Ezekiel's incomparable boneyard.

The sleeper murmurs to himself; he has
a sense of how far darkness radiates,
taking care of its own. It troubles him,
his sleep. The dreamcatcher, settled,
picks up the smallest wisp of dismay,
of possible deflection from the arcs
of joy he would follow, releasing it
into the smoke and mirrors of its own
absorption. Through his window at night
he sees stars, pieces of the Big Dipper
but nothing else he could cobble together
into a clear shape. Sometimes when he looks through
the dreamcatcher he can't tell the drops
from the starscrabble, his pupils relaxing,
his vision becoming the mesh, the angel wings,
the best dreams shimmering in the malachite.

THE LIGHT THE MAGICIAN

The magician is
sawing light in half, his sheer,
importunate spell

meshed in the brilliant,
cardiovascular net-
body suspended

in air before him.
A writhe of pain or supple
ecstasy shivers

through it, a blind name
he hums, his blade caresses.
Out here, we are screened

only by the mist
that sheathes them, incandescent,
each making a play

for its mate. The saw
hovers in the shimmering
light; the magician

feels the bright music
climb his arm into his mind.
Just as he lets go,

the saw explodes, *poof*,
into the finest dust – stunned,
aloof. The light holds

everything as we
watch everything merge into
one lovely bow, sweep-

ing its coattails back,
its top hat in a semi-
circle like the edge

of a broadaxe blade
toward us. The sigh of terror
and relief that joins

the dispersing light
could as well be its breathing
as ours, finally

released, time's aura
and echo whispering each
other's semblances.

Our applause rises,
as if in this rickety
hall it would fashion

a new renaissance
of domes, shadowing in them
history's next sweet

cherubim of fire.

REFRAIN

1.

When they are spirits of the past themselves,
they meet, *sans* everything, hearts on fire
for nothing, all schema hung out to dry,
flapping randomly in the neverair,
items in Joan's discarded canvases.

It feels like a liberation. Why
else would they be everywhere and nowhere,
bodiless yet present, unable to speak
yet full of words in a littered exosphere
where only their non-echoes can reply

to their longing? Nothing can contradict
a wild surmise, or a fractious hint,
or a practical fitting together of lenses
by shaped explosion finding implosion out.
There was no longer a point of impact

for either conflicting theories or tenses
of personality – one a shrewd bearbrunt
bulldozer, the other a master
of withdrawal and trenchant motherwit.
They overlook their mountain's charred expanses.

In this fluttering aftermath of disaster,
boneless and blown, Oppie's implausible hat
and Groves' dress brocade are as anonymous
as a dreamcatcher's feather in the void,
minuscule detritus left to pester

the stars. *What if? What if?* A soft chorus
of unstrung tunings hovers, its kinetic hum
like willow leaves floating in a soft wind.
They could be near the direst vacuum
if we could measure where they are, their afflatus

dispersed so finely in the nanoseconds
of minus time. The fall of a sparrow,
summer's fading, the bland eye of an empty
dryer, a jumprope's tick, the blade's furrow
parching, unseeded – through these one reckons

phases in a declension. Cacophony,
too, despite itself, needs time, a mere extreme.
But Leslie R. and J. Robert lack a place
you can call a place. Their fondest dream
is no longer *fact*, but *now*. Humpty Dumpty,

Ozymandias, the Seven Cities
of Troy, bog bones still hidden from old Zeke,
seem paradise beside this feckless drift,
this rinse of neverair. If they could speak
is as extraneous as ice

and numbers are pawns in a cosmic grift
that makes God's dice little more than jacks
thrown on a stoop. *Who would have thought?* becomes
a strain in the hanging music,
inaudible but for its inmost gift:

2.

the neverair sings to itself, consumes
and nourishes less than nothing falling
open and away, rangeless, the filters
of starfall, light chaining until light's all
shatters past them, meeting without words
or scheme, not even the imponderable
galactic crawl toward itself, toward fire

that boils more fire, a grace of flames
spun in the unhearkened telling
gone, webs without a weave, shelters
of windless inclination, knell
unwinding departure inwards,
a likelihood kept unstable
by its own luminous absence of air.

3.

They would assert themselves.
Of course. They would light a fire
in the numberless cold. *Dry*
is an essence within air
replacing air; spaces

become space. They don't ask why
nothing ignites, why *nowhere*
is the language they speak
in the flecked exosphere
that gives neither reply

nor echo, or contradicts
their being a lost hint
of themselves, lenses
of lightfade so thinned out
you could breathe them. *Impact*

and *float* are synonyms, tenses
time's spume. They bear the brunt
of weightlessness; they master
arts that require neither wit
nor dexterity. Expanses

that once dwarfed them, disaster
looming, like Oppie's hat
become as anonymous
as a speck in their new void.
Where colleagues used to pester

them – *what if? what if?* a chorus
of exhaustion – a feathered hum
now shadows their hearing, spacewind
just out of earshot, a vacuum
beckoning one afflatus

to join another. Seconds
vanish into it sparrow-
quick[n], yet it stays empty,
a bottomless furrow,
seedless. If one reckons

the mind's polyphony
as evolution's extreme
achievement, this is the place-
less place to test that dream.
Not even Humpty Dumpty

applies; the leveling of cities
is an image old Zeke
doesn't pursue: the drift
of bone dust refutes him. To speak
in the tongues of outer space

requires we bypass the gift
of sound and matter, take
to heart the fate that becomes
us, the nuclear music
ghosting the traces we have left.

MONKS 5

He sees things as if words
inhere in them and he can assist them
in their emergence
to light and air, their mime,
their vacant choreography.
They aren't in any sense *his* words.
It is a passage in trust, a marking.
This caretaking is not his either
but it is everything to him,
the nearest thing to his mind,
a gift he does not put down
no matter the faded texts,
their erasure, or his own.

THE EXPANDING UNIVERSE

The universe has a curious
geometry that denies the existence
of either a centre or an edge.
                    – Ian Redpath

– the mind's great whirl, its curvilinear
siftings, the spherical web it throws out
into its shapeless dark, a comfort
and a confusion, vaster than its own
intentions, its need. Galaxies spun
and forgotten in the wake of new ones
drift, centripetal, along their austere
tracks, aimless after their first inception.

– or another figure, the mind as conductor,
its baton seeking to harmonize
the discrete, far-floating systems, gone,
their inevitable musics tuned
only to their disparate motions, their space.
Not even the magic inherent
in that little wand could draw this spreading
composition back into the light
of its original impulse, its rounding out.

So they expand, these motes, nuggets
and feral gasses the imagination
spins out and off into the neverair,
angels of like subsistence, threading,
lines of their own inherence, shapes shifting.
I make, and am present among, them
somehow in the distances widening –
a nonentity, a spread of time.

DECLENSIONS

Robert Frost's son killed his father
many times and himself once.
Hart Crane jumped from the back end
of a ship into the sea's wide spindrift
gaze, into the sea's rapt bulk.
Mother Teresa and other nomads
don't eat much and my friend Floyd says *dirigible*
when he means *stone*. Unmoored, and the tide
is ebbing, stranding its hem.

Another poet began once *Light breaks*
where no sun shines, an anatomical
paradox and miracle of some import
to the continuance of the species.
The anonymous masons who erected
the cathedral at Rheims imagined the grain
in the stone, one stone at a time,
and Michaelangelo quarried his own marble,
in Carrara – the magic word, alight –
seeing in this block or that, scattered,
the shape of bone and sinew, the caress of air
around an iris, a thigh, a fingernail.

A harpoon aloft in the whaler's dream
finds a reef of blubber that floats him dawnward
on the keel of sleep. He is divorced
from the widow of his waking.
Likewise the hermit and the hermit crab
keep mum, fathering who knows what
leaps of faith in their traceless abandonment.
Men of the world know nothing of this
though they are variously stranded, too,
busy with patricide, up to their hilts
in the blindness of generation.

Stars burn, and burn out. The Hourglass Nova
cools and dims. In a few thousand years
the bright gasses hooping its haunted eye
will fade and disperse, leaving a white dot
in the cosmos, an ember, also waning.
Out there gravity may be a lens, bending
light. A cluster galaxy can distort
the fire light years beyond it into arcs
tracing its own dark matter, its deeper field.

MUMMERY

He vigorously asserted
the reality of the unseen world.
– Max Perutz on Max Planck

Years of continuous labor
producing a shape in air that shifted
daily, almost imperceptibly, seeking
who knows what intimate configuration,
perhaps something as abstract as a number:
the sound of the soul measuring its dance
into light. Or nothing,
our nuclear friend. Is it an ornate pride,
a Ptolemaic tic, that we imagine
the light of a star as coming toward us,
or having any direction at all?
What could be more indifferent than this pen,
warmed by my fingers, when I put it down?

BLACK HOLES

All the yonic yawns that inhere in this subject
belong to other ruminations and will not appear here.
Instead, the poster says, observe the various torques,
molecular time,
compression not even the most
accomplished lyric poet guessed,
how the universe forks
and forks, spills into itself, and doesn't rhyme,

how the ghosts take forever to appear and disappear,
leaving nothing but whispers that lead us to suspect
and nominate and theorize
about what might have been there
once, and isn't. Attraction one,
a series of gaseous centers
drunk with light, shows the sure sign
of a black hole is its bright enterprise,

its dazzling maw, a galaxy's digestive track
consuming and belching, all process, a plummet of sheer
combustion. In the adjacent aisle
Centaurus A
tilts in its homey
approximation of an eye
stitched out with vitreous
floaters, spider style.

Next door, Andromeda, flanked by two satellites,
presents its pale yolk and sizzled fringe, a cannibal
dying of its own appetite,
the drastic, crawling fate
even of the sweet Milky Way,
its Orion Arm nestling the planet
we are nourished by.
The rest of the display –

Berenice sleeping, Carina, the Whirlpool,
Dorado, Sculptor, assorted classical acts –
overwhelms the diminished visitor
of the species we are most
fond of, leaving it lethargic,
disoriented, at the core
burned down, a depressed wreck
capable only of staring at ghost

images flickering on the front pane of a box.
On my wife's sewing machine bobbin and spool
feed their needle, its slow
and rapid tickings making a rhythm
less predictable than Penelope's
at her loom, but a constant flow
nonetheless on the wide fathom
of space's steep entropy.

The TV screen and the stitching are both hypnotic;
the wayward sailor's wife remembers to exhale
as her shuttle slides through the warp,
and she can undo what she does;
from the machine a hemmed panel
of bright cloth eases – so our sleep
sews memory and dream, the rise
of being. Nothing is final

but repetition, the rehearsals of appetite
and gravity spinning and unspinning in neverair.
Name the new names, conjure
umbrellas where there is no moisture,
bless the monks' bowed gesture, evoke the magician
and his inky smoke, call up
from the drasty deep
echoes of Magog and Leviathan.

Litanies of spite
and counter spite reel and unreel;
tongues flap their blame and praise,
their coups and coos;
organs rise, beget, and melt
quicker than sighs.
It's as silent out there among the cataracts
as generation, as the movement of glaciers.

Once upon a time before the future is a speck
of leftover cinder from our seared planet,
all the figures we have dressed
the stars and their spaces with
may peel off and drift
toward us – an instant of bare sight,
of unlending. Our eyes may devour this, impressed
at last with their own blind light.

Pinyon Publishing
978-0-9821561-1-7

Pinyon Publishing
978-0-9821561-1-7

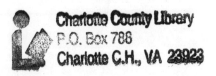

Printed in the United States
148884LV00009B/191/P